HAL•LEONARD INSTRUMENTAL PLAY-ALONG

AUDIO ACCESS INCLUDED

PLAYBACK+
eed • Pitch • Balance • Loop

Peaceful Hymns

T0085248

Audio arrangements by Peter Deneff

To access audio visit:
www.halleonard.com/mylibrary
Enter Code
3519-1311-0337-7162

ISBN 978-1-70513-789-5

HAL•LEONARD®

Visit Hal Leonard Online at
www.halleonard.com

Contact us:
Hal Leonard
7777 West Bluemound Road
Milwaukee, WI 53213
Email: info@halleonard.com

In Europe, contact:
Hal Leonard Europe Limited
42 Wigmore Street
Marylebone, London, W1U 2RN
Email: info@halleonardeurope.com

In Australia, contact:
Hal Leonard Australia Pty. Ltd.
4 Lentara Court
Cheltenham, Victoria, 3192 Australia
Email: info@halleonard.com.au

ABIDE WITH ME

FLUTE

Music by WILLIAM H. MONK

ALL CREATURES OF OUR GOD AND KING

FLUTE

Music from *Geistliche Kirchengesang*

Slowly, with reverence

ALL HAIL THE POWER OF JESUS' NAME

FLUTE

Music by OLIVER HOLDEN

ALL THROUGH THE NIGHT

FLUTE

Welsh Folksong

AMAZING GRACE

FLUTE

Traditional American Melody

BE THOU MY VISION

FLUTE

Traditional Irish

BLESSED ASSURANCE

FLUTE

Music by PHOEBE PALMER KNAPP

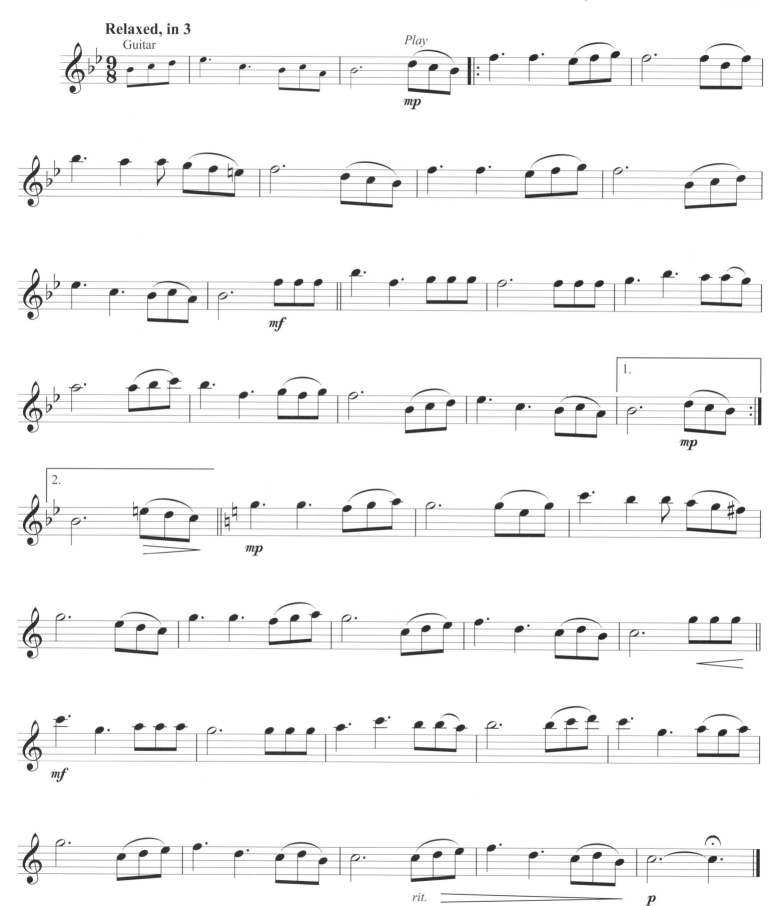

COME, THOU FOUNT OF EVERY BLESSING

FLUTE

Music from John Wyeth's *Repository of Sacred Music*

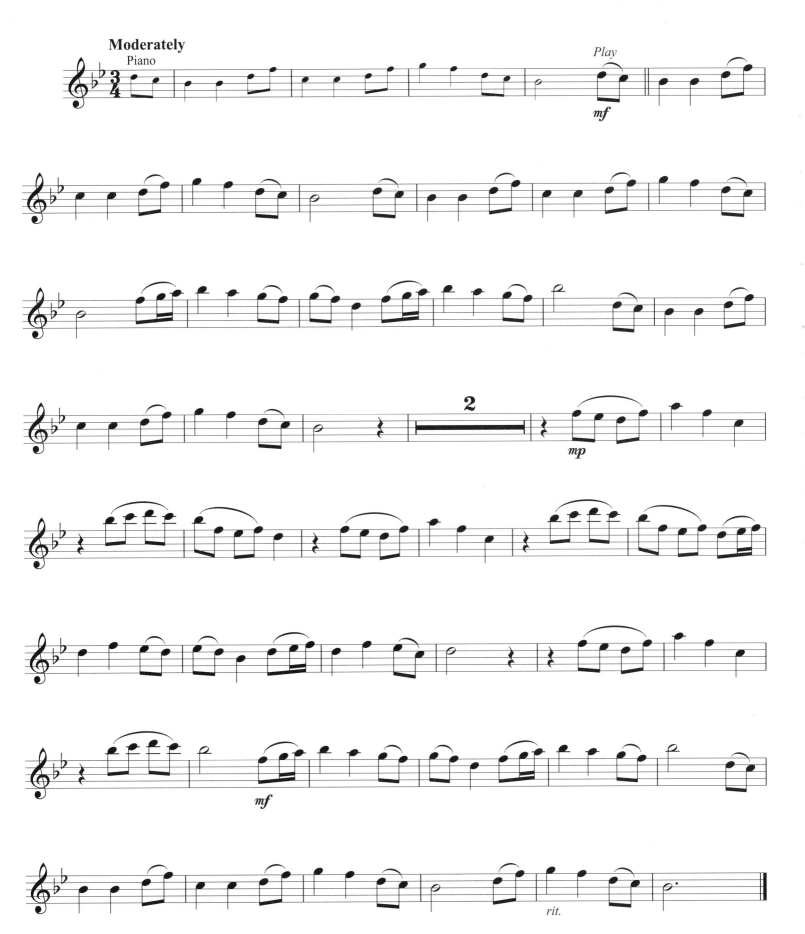

FAIREST LORD JESUS

FLUTE

Music from *Schlesische Volkslieder*

FOR THE BEAUTY OF THE EARTH

FLUTE

Music by CONRAD KOCHER

GREAT IS THY FAITHFULNESS

FLUTE

Music by WILLIAM M. RUNYAN

HOLY, HOLY, HOLY

FLUTE

Music by JOHN B. DYKES

HOW FIRM A FOUNDATION

FLUTE

Traditional music compiled by JOSEPH FUNK

rit.

I NEED THEE EVERY HOUR

FLUTE

Music by ROBERT LOWRY

IT IS WELL WITH MY SOUL

FLUTE

Music by PHILIP P. BLISS

JUST AS I AM

FLUTE

Music by WILLIAM B. BRADBURY

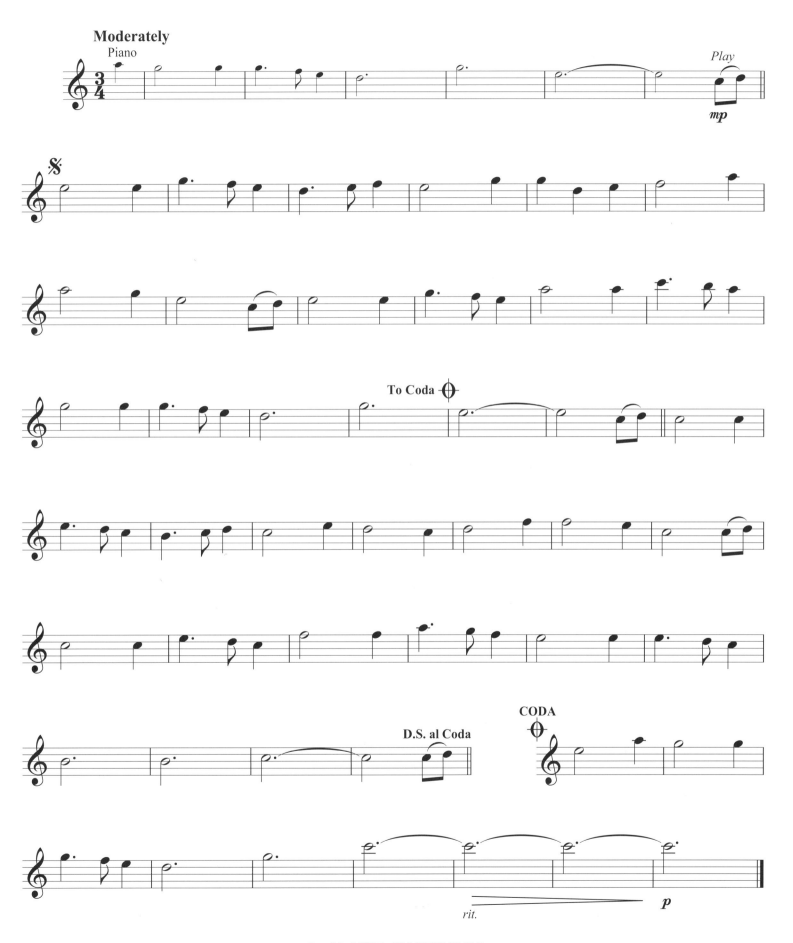

THE KING OF LOVE MY SHEPHERD IS

FLUTE

Traditional Irish Melody

LET ALL MORTAL FLESH KEEP SILENCE

FLUTE

17th Century French Carol

MY FAITH LOOKS UP TO THEE

FLUTE

Music by LOWELL MASON

NEARER, MY GOD, TO THEE

FLUTE

Music by LOWELL MASON

WERE YOU THERE WHEN THEY CRUCIFIED MY LORD?

FLUTE

Traditional

WHAT A FRIEND WE HAVE IN JESUS

FLUTE

Music by CHARLES C. CONVERSE

WONDROUS LOVE

FLUTE

Southern American Folk Hymn